Workbook

World Link

Developing English Fluency

1

HEINLE
CENGAGE Learning™

Australia • Brazil • Japan • Korea • Mexico • Singapore • Spain • United Kingdom • United States

HEINLE
CENGAGE Learning

World Link 1 Workbook
2nd Edition

Publisher: Sherrise Roehr

Senior Development Editor:
Jennifer Meldrum

Senior Development Editor:
Katherine Carroll

Director of Global Marketing:
Ian Martin

Senior Product Marketing Manager:
Katie Kelley

Assistant Marketing Manager:
Anders Bylund

Content Project Manager:
John Sarantakis

Senior Print Buyer:
Mary Beth Hennebury

Composition: Pre-Press PMG

Cover/Text Design: Page2 LLC

Cover Image: iStockphoto

ISBN-13: 978-1-4240-6576-9
ISBN-10: 1-4240-6576-3

Heinle
20 Channel Center Street
Boston, MA 02210
USA

Cengage Learning is a leading provider of customized learning solutions with office locations around the globe, including Singapore, the United Kingdom, Australia, Mexico, Brazil, and Japan. Locate our local office at:
international.cengage.com/region

Cengage Learning products are represented in Canada by Nelson Education, Ltd.

Visit Heinle online at **elt.heinle.com**
Visit our corporate website at **cengage.com**

Printed in the United States of America
4 5 6 7 8 9 10 - 14

Photo Credits

Unit 2: page 8: Comstock Images/Jupiter Images; page 13: Robert Adrian Hillman, 2009/Used under license from Shutterstock.com

Unit 3: page 19: Dmitriy Shironosov, 2009/Used under license from Shutterstock.com

Unit 4: page 23: PhotoDisc/Getty Images

Unit 5: page 26: PhotoDisc/Getty Images; page 28 Popperfoto/Getty Images; page 30: Tim Graham/Alamy

Unit 6: page 33: PhotoDisc/Getty Images

Unit 7: page 42 top and bottom: PhotoDisc/Getty Images; page 43: oksana.perkins, 2009/Used under license from Shutterstock.com

Unit 8: page 46: i love images/Jupiter Images; page 48 top, center, bottom: PhotoDisc/Getty Images

Unit 9: page 51: PhotoDisc/Getty Images; page 54: poco_bw/istockphoto.com

Unit 10: page 56: Denisa V, 2009/Used under license from Shutterstock.com; page 61: Oliwkowyga/Dreamstime.com

Unit 11: page 62: Kozlovskaya Ksenia, 2009/Used under license from Shutterstock.com; page 64: Kokhanchikov/Used under license from Shutterstock.com; page 67: SFC, 2009/Used under license from Shutterstock.com

Unit 12: page 68: teacept, 2009/Used under license from Shutterstock.com; page 70: Losevsky Pavel, 2009/Used under license from Shutterstock.com

Scope & Sequence

1 Vocabulary Workout

A Complete the form with your own information. Draw your picture in the box.

International Friendship Club

New Member Form

First name _____

Last name _____

Hometown _____

Cell number _____

E-mail address _____

Languages _____

Interests _____

_____

_____

_____

B Match the questions with the answers.

1. __d__ What's your name?
2. _____ Do you speak English?
3. _____ Where are you from?
4. _____ Where do you live now?
5. _____ What's your e-mail address?
6. _____ How old are you?
7. _____ What do you do?
8. _____ What do you do for fun?

a. I'm from Japan.
b. I'm a student.
c. Keiko333@*memail.com
d. Keiko Goto.
e. I'm 20.
f. Yes, I do.
g. I like to travel.
h. I live in Los Angeles.

2 Conversation Workout

A Number the conversation to put it in order.

_____ Yeah. I study art at Hunter College.

____1____ Hi. My name is David. I'm in apartment B-10.

_____ What do you do, Anna?

_____ Nice to meet you, too.

_____ So, are you a student, David?

_____ That's interesting.

_____ I'm a student at NYU. I also work in a restaurant.

_____ Hi, David. I'm Anna. I'm in C-6. It's nice to meet you.

B Write conversations with a friend and a family member.

1. Conversation with a friend

You: _____

_____: _____

You: _____

_____: _____

You: _____

_____: _____

You: _____

_____: _____

2. Conversation with a family member

You: _____

_____: _____

You: _____

_____: _____

You: _____

_____: _____

You: _____

_____: _____

3 Language Workout

A What do these people do for fun? Fill in the spaces for *YOU*. Then write sentences. Follow the example.

✓ = yes   ✗ = no

	Jason	Cristina	Sue and Ann	YOU
Go dancing	✓	✗	✓	___
Watch TV	✗	✓	✓	___
Write e-mail	✓	✓	✗	___
Play tennis	✗	✓	✓	___

1 Jason *goes dancing.*
He *doesn't watch TV.*
He *writes e-mail.*
He *doesn't play tennis.*

2 Cristina _____
_____
_____
_____

3 Sue and Ann _____
_____
_____
_____

4 _____
_____
_____
_____

B Match the questions and the answers.

1. Do they have a child? _____
2. Is Ms. Baker your teacher? _____
3. Are you from Mexico? _____
4. Is Mr. Lee your teacher? _____
5. Are the new students from China? _____
6. Do you speak Spanish? _____
7. Does your mother work? _____
8. Does your father have a car? _____

a. No, she isn't.
b. Yes, I do.
c. No, he doesn't.
d. Yes, they do.
e. Yes, he is.
f. Yes, she does.
g. No, I'm not.
h. No, they aren't.

C Unscramble the words to make correct questions. Then write true answers.

1. (you / do / where / live) _____?
_____

2. (TV / when / do / watch / you) _____?
_____

3. (live / who / you / with / do) _____?
_____

4. (weekends / you / what / do / do / on) _____?
_____

5. (English / do / you / study / where) _____?
_____

Lesson B What does he look like?

1 Vocabulary and Language Workout

A Write the words in the correct box. Then circle the words that describe you.

blue	young	blond	thin	long	heavy-set
straight	slim	green	average height	gray	spiky
elderly	tall	curly	average weight	red	

Age	Height	Weight	Hair color	Hairstyle	Eye color
_____	_____	_____	_____	_____	_____
_____	_____	_____	_____	_____	_____
		_____	_____	_____	
				_____	

B Write sentences about you.

1. _____
2. _____
3. _____

C Describe these people.

1. Liz *She* _____
   _____
   _____

2. Ed _____
   _____
   _____

3. Ana _____
   _____
   _____

2 Reading and Writing

A Read these e-mail messages.

1

http://www.mail*.net/compose.html

📁 INBOX   ✉ REPLY   ✉ REPLY ALL   ✉➡ FORWARD   ✖ DELETE

Date: April 16   Subject: Mr. Ryder's visit

Dear Mr. Peters,

Please meet Mr. James Ryder at the airport at 11:00 tomorrow. His flight is UA238 from Los Angeles. He is a tall man in his sixties with gray hair, and he wears big glasses. His meeting with the Marketing Department is at 4:00. Thank you.

Kyra Greene
Marketing Department

2

http://www.mail*.net/compose.html

📁 INBOX   ✉ REPLY   ✉ REPLY ALL   ✉➡ FORWARD   ✖ DELETE

Date: April 16   Subject: Plans for tomorrow

Hi Karen,

Thanks so much for meeting my brother at the airport tomorrow. Please tell him I finish work at 3:00. His name is David, he's 32, and he looks a lot like me (short, heavyset, clean-shaven, curly brown hair). He's coming at 11:00 on flight AA397 from Toronto. Let's have dinner tomorrow night!

See you!

Rick

3

http://www.mail*.net/compose.html

📁 INBOX   ✉ REPLY   ✉ REPLY ALL   ✉➡ FORWARD   ✖ DELETE

Date: April 16   Subject: Car problems again!

Gina—

HELP! Can you meet my friend Tom at the airport tomorrow? My car has big problems and I can't drive it. Tom is coming on flight KX661 from Denver at 11:00. He's average height and kind of thin, with long blond hair and a mustache. Thanks a million!

Chris

B Look at this picture. Write the number of the e-mail message in the correct circle. There are three extra circles.

C Read and complete the descriptions with *has, have, is, are, wear,* or *wears.*

My favorite actor is Maria Rios. She _____ short, black hair. She _____ average height. She _____ big blue eyes and she doesn't _____ glasses. She _____ very young. I think she _____ in her twenties.

My favorite singers are the Bell Tones. They _____ in their thirties. They _____ all tall and thin. They _____ long blond hair and they _____ big glasses.

D Now write a description of a famous person.

_____

_____

_____

_____

_____

_____

_____

_____

_____

_____

1 Vocabulary Workout

A Unscramble these verbs.

1. lakt _____

2. abrk _____

3. stuoh _____

4. elims _____

5. kool _____

6. tipno _____

7. its _____

8. evaw _____

B Circle the correct answer.

1. She is (sitting / pointing) at the TV.

2. He is looking (at / to) his friend.

3. The dog is (talking / barking).

4. They are not happy. They are (shouting / smiling).

5. I am sitting (on / at) a chair.

6. She sees her brother. She is (waving / looking) to him.

C Complete the sentences. Use the verb in parentheses.

1. (look) She's _____ at the man.

2. (smile) I'm _____ at my friend.

3. (bark) The dog's _____ at Jim.

4. (shout) He's _____ at the dog.

5. (sit) We're _____ in class right now.

6. (point) They're _____ at the car.

2 Conversation Workout

A Write each word in the correct box.

great	not bad	stressed	pretty good
tired	fine	not so good	unhappy

I feel good. ☺	I feel OK. ☻	I feel bad. ☹

B Complete the sentences. Use your own ideas.

1. **Barbara:** Hi, Lisa. _____

   Lisa: _____

   Barbara: Great! _____

   Lisa: Not so good.

   Barbara: _____

   Lisa: I'm _____. I have to go to the dentist tomorrow.

   Barbara: _____

2. **Carlos:** Hi, Rick.

   Rick: _____

   Carlos: Great! _____

   Rick: _____

   Carlos: _____

   Rick: I'm _____. My brother used my car and had a big accident.

   Carlos: _____

3. **Shauna:** Hi, Jeff.

   Jeff: _____

   Shauna: I'm kind of tired. _____

   Jeff: I'm doing great! _____

   Shauna: I'm happy for you. _____

   Jeff: Sounds good!

3 Language Workout

A What are they doing? Write sentences. Follow the example.

Example: ~~Pat / plan~~   a sofa

1. My sister / talk to   TV
2. I / sit on   ~~a trip~~
3. They / watch   the phone
4. Lee / talk on   her friend

Example: _Pat is planning a trip._ _____

1. _____
2. _____
3. _____
4. _____

B Complete the sentences.

Paula: So, Jane, what (1. you, do) _____ these days?

Jane: I (2. work) _____ in an office. And I (3. study) _____ computer science in the evening.

Paula: You're really busy!

Jane: That's for sure! And in my free time, I (4. learn) _____ Spanish for my vacation. I (5. plan) _____ a trip to Mexico.

Paula: What about your brothers? How (6. they, do) _____?

Jane: They (7. do) _____ great! Alex (8. help) _____ our father in his business, and Adam (9. go) _____ to Pacific University.

C What are they doing now? Write true sentences about you, your family, and your friends.

Example: _My mother is working now._ _____

1. _____
2. _____
3. _____
4. _____
5. _____

Lesson B Body language and gestures

1 Vocabulary and Language Workout

A Write the letter of the correct answer.

1. Can I have that coat? I'm _____.
   a. excited
   b. cold
   c. confident

2. He's shouting. I think he's _____.
   a. angry
   b. bored
   c. confused

3. I have no money for lunch. I'm _____.
   a. confident
   b. hot
   c. embarrassed

4. She's sleeping at the movies. She's _____.
   a. thirsty
   b. bored
   c. excited

B Match the sentence halves. Write the letter of the answer on the line.

1. To say "I don't know," _____   a. you use one finger.
2. For good luck, _____   b. you are hungry.
3. To point to something, _____   c. you are bored.
4. To call someone, _____   d. you shrug your shoulders.
5. If you are not afraid, _____   e. you are confident.
6. If you want to eat, _____   f. you are confused.
7. If a TV show isn't any good, _____ g. you cross your fingers.
8. If you don't understand, _____   h. you use your hand.

C Write the correct answer. Use the words in the box.

me you him her it us them

1. I like Maria. I see _____ every day.
2. The teacher is angry with you and me. She is shouting at _____.
3. You are my best friend. I like _____ a lot.
4. You have my keys. Please give _____ to me.
5. I am planning a trip to Paris. I am happy about _____.
6. My son is on vacation. I am writing a letter to _____.

2 Reading and Writing

A Read this article about gestures in three countries.

TRAVEL ASIA 🌐

Know Before You Go!

> **Bangladesh**
People greet their friends by shaking hands softly and then putting their hands over their hearts. People in Bangladesh don't use many gestures. Waving at people and winking are very rude. Don't touch people on the head. Don't point with your foot—Bangladeshi people think feet are very dirty.

> **Indonesia**
Indonesians greet people with a long handshake, and they bow at the same time. At a meeting, give every person your business card, but use your right hand—using your left hand is very rude.

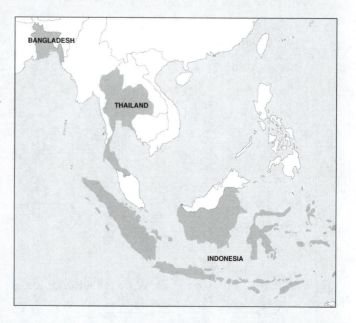

> **Thailand**
In Thailand, the traditional greeting is called *wai*—people put their hands together and bow. Men and women don't often touch each other in public. Thai people don't use their hands for gestures, but they love to smile a lot. They sometimes laugh when they feel nervous or embarrassed.

B Put checks (✓) in the correct boxes.

	Bangladesh	Indonesia	Thailand
1. People shake hands.			
2. People bow.			
3. People give business cards.			
4. There are rules about touching.			
5. Don't wave at people here.			
6. There aren't many hand gestures.			
7. People don't wink.			
8. Don't use your left hand here.			

C Read the paragraph and circle the correct answer.

My country is the United Arab Emirates. (1. We / Us) have some special gestures. When two men meet, (2. they / them) shake hands. Sometimes old men touch their noses together. Women kiss (3. their / them) friends on the cheek. If a man meets a woman, he doesn't shake hands with (4. she / her). (5. He / Him) just smiles. When you give your friend a drink or a paper, give it to (6. he / him) with your right hand. Don't use your left hand. And don't point at people with your finger. Use your hand to gesture towards (7. they / them).

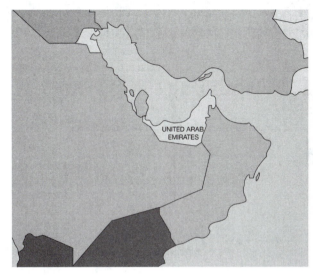

D Write about gestures in your country.

_____

_____

_____

_____

_____

_____

_____

_____

_____

_____

_____

What Do We Need?

Lesson A At the supermarket

1 Vocabulary Workout

A Unscramble these food words.

1. sehece _____
2. nickche _____
3. primsh _____
4. trubet _____
5. troguy _____

6. mootat _____
7. torcar _____
8. slednoo _____
9. nnaaab _____
10. lappe _____

B Cross out the one that's different.

Example: apple ~~shrimp~~ grapes banana

1. chips	soda	cake	chicken
2. yogurt	rice	ice cream	butter
3. soda	orange juice	banana	milk
4. beef	salad	lettuce	tomato
5. instant noodles	chips	French fries	tofu
6. organic food	junk food	fresh food	healthy food

C Complete the chart. Use foods from this unit and other foods you know.

Foods I like 😊	Foods that are OK 😐	Foods I don't like 😞

2 Conversation Workout

A Number the conversation to put it in order.

_____ Okay. What about frozen foods?

_____ We need some drinks. Buy soda and orange juice.

_____ Okay. I'm going to the store. See you later.

____1____ I'm making a shopping list for the class party. We have cake. What else do we need?

_____ We don't need any. We have frozen shrimp and ground beef.

B Now write three new conversations.

1. **Jim:** _____

   Ellen: _____

   Jim: _____

   Ellen: _____

   Jim: _____

Barbecue
beef, shrimp
potatoes, carrots
dessert: grapes, oranges

Graduation Party
chicken, fish
lettuce, tomatoes
soda, bottled water

2. **Toshi:** _____

   Leo: _____

   Toshi: _____

   Leo: _____

   Toshi: _____

3. **You:** _____

   Your friend: _____

   You: _____

   Your friend: _____

   You: _____

3 Language Workout

A What's on the table? Write the count and noncount items in the correct list.

Count: *three apples* _____

_____

_____

_____

Noncount: *some grapes* _____

_____

_____

_____

B Fill in *some* or *any*.

1. I want to buy _____ new books.

2. Do you have _____ brothers or sisters?

3. Jose is reading _____ interesting books.

4. My city has _____ very old buildings.

5. Do you want _____ ice cream?

6. There aren't _____ mountains in my country.

7. Please get _____ soap at the drugstore.

8. Does Mrs. Yoon have _____ children?

9. I can't make a cake. There aren't _____ eggs.

10. Can I have _____ milk, please?

C Rewrite the sentences. Correct one mistake in each sentence.

1. I'm sorry. I don't have some money with me today.

_____

2. We have some tomatoes and some lettuces for the salad.

_____

3. I'll go to the store and buy any soda.

_____

4. Do we have some soap in the bathroom?

_____

5. Are there any potato on the table?

_____

Lesson B Let's go shopping!

1 Vocabulary and Language Workout

A Circle the correct answer.

1. I need a big (shop / shopping) bag.

2. There is a food (shop / shopping) at the (shop / shopping) center.

3. Where do you (shop / shopping)?

4. I (shop / shopping) around for low prices.

5. Let's go to a coffee (shop / shopping).

6. We like to go window (shop / shopping).

B Write the letter of the correct answer.

1. There are _____ toys in the room.
   a. some
   b. any
   c. much

2. I have _____ clothing.
   a. any
   b. much
   c. a lot of

3. There isn't _____ milk in the glass.
   a. some
   b. much
   c. many

4. There aren't _____ students in this class.
   a. some
   b. much
   c. many

5. There isn't _____ salad on the table.
   a. any
   b. a lot of
   c. many

6. There is _____ butter on the bread.
   a. any
   b. some
   c. much

C Write sentences about yourself. Use *some, any, much, many,* or *a lot of.*

Examples: magazines – I have *a lot of* magazines.   newspapers – I don't have *any* newspapers.

1. T-shirts _____

2. close friends _____

3. jewelry _____

4. books in English _____

5. extra money _____

2 Reading and Writing

A Read the shopping guide.

SHOPPING GUIDE

(1.) Metro Department Store

Prices: $$$$$ **Service:** ☺☺☺☺☺

Metro Department Store is very modern. It's a great place for electronics. There are a lot of cool new cameras, cell phones, and even computers. You can buy many things for your house. The clothes are great, but the prices are crazy! Everything is very expensive, but the clerks are very friendly and helpful.

(2.) Gracy's Department Store

Prices: $$ **Service:** ☺☺

Gracy's Department Store has some nice clothes for your parents, but there aren't many things for young people. The prices are quite low. Don't shop for electronics here, there are just a few cameras, and there aren't any TVs or computers. The music department is great. They have a lot of new rock CDs, and they also have some jazz and world music.

(3.) The Little Shop of Sales

Prices: $ **Service:** ☺☺☺

The Little Shop of Sales isn't like most stores. They don't sell new items. Their stuff is "like new" or "gently used." They sell only clothing and furniture. However, you won't find any junk here. If you don't have a lot of spending money, this is the place for you. Come early on Saturday mornings before all the good stuff is gone.

B Skim the shopping guide. Then write the number of each store in front of the correct title.

_____ A good place to buy inexpensive items

_____ A good place to buy electronics

_____ A good place to buy CDs

C Circle *T* for *true* and *F* for *false*. Rewrite the false sentences to make them true.

Example: T   (F)   The Little Shop of Sales has high prices.

The Little Shop of Sales has low prices.

_____

1.   T   F   Gracy's has a lot of clothing for young people.

_____

2.   T   F   You can buy a computer at the Little Shop of Sales.

_____

3.   T   F   Metro has a good electronics department.

_____

4.   T   F   Gracy's has low prices.

_____

5.   T   F   Metro sells a lot of CDs.

_____

D Write about your favorite store. What do they sell? How are the prices? What do you buy there?

_____

_____

_____

_____

_____

_____

_____

_____

_____

_____

_____

4 Vacation!

Lesson A How's the weather?

1 Vocabulary Workout

A Match the questions with the answers.

1. __d__ The sky is blue when the weather is   a. warm.

2. _____ If you are a little cold, you are   b. cloudy.

3. _____ If the weather is a little windy, it is   c. breezy.

4. _____ Just before it rains, the sky becomes   d. sunny.

5. _____ If you feel a little hot, you feel   e. dry.

6. _____ The ground is white when the weather is   f. chilly.

7. _____ If it doesn't rain, the weather is   g. wet.

8. _____ If it is raining, the streets are   h. snowy.

B Complete the sentences with the words from the box.

foggy	partly	strong	snowy	warm

1. Today the sky is _____ cloudy.

2. There are _____ winds today.

3. Today the temperature is _____.

4. I can't see the sky because it is _____ today.

5. It can be _____ when the weather is very cold.

C Complete the chart. Use weather words from the unit and other weather words you know.

Examples: rainy weather, warm breezes

I don't like it. 😞	It's OK. 😐	I like it. 😊

2 Conversation Workout

A Match the words to make correct expressions.

1. Good __d__   a. I will.

2. I don't _____   b. right.

3. OK, _____   c. OK.

4. I'd rather _____   d. idea.

5. You're probably _____   e. not.

6. I think I'll be _____   f. think so.

B Use the sentences in the box to make a conversation.

Oh, yeah. You're probably right.	Really? Why not?
It's snowing hard and the roads aren't safe.	Well, I don't think you should drive.
Yeah. Sure.	Are you planning to go?

Carlos: Tina's having a party tonight.

Anna: _____

Carlos: _____

Anna: _____

Carlos: _____

Anna: _____

Carlos: _____

C Now write a new conversation. Give a friend some advice.

A friend: _____

You: _____

A friend: _____

You: _____

A friend: _____

You: _____

3 Language Workout

A Match the sentence parts. Write the letter of the answer on the line.

1. Rita loves soccer, __c__   a. but she doesn't have any sisters.

2. She can watch a video, _____   b. or she can eat at a restaurant.

3. Her computer doesn't work, _____   c. but she doesn't like baseball.

4. It's hot in summer, _____   d. so she always takes the bus.

5. She can't drive a car, _____   e. but she can't speak French.

6. She has three brothers, _____   f. so she's getting a new one.

7. She can cook at home, _____   g. or she can listen to music.

8. She speaks Spanish, _____   h. so she always wears T-shirts.

B Put the sentences together with *or, so,* or *but.*

1. It's really cold today. It's very sunny.

   _____

2. Should I wear a dress to the party? Should I wear pants?

   _____

3. Kevin likes dogs. He doesn't like cats.

   _____

4. We have a test tomorrow. I'm studying this afternoon.

   _____

5. My computer is old. I really like it.

   _____

6. We can have fish for dinner. We can have chicken.

   _____

7. It's raining today. We're staying home.

   _____

C Finish the sentences using *or, so,* or *but.* Use your own ideas.

Example: I like fish, *but I don't like chicken.* _____

1. I'm studying English, _____

2. I know many English words, _____

3. Today I can _____

4. I like _____

5. I have _____

Lesson B On vacation

1 Vocabulary and Language Workout

A Complete the sentences. Use a word from the box.

buy	check	get	go
pack	rent	show	take

1. We need to _____ a car.

2. You can _____ a passport at the post office.

3. They plan to _____ sightseeing in New York City.

4. I have to _____ my suitcase.

5. I _____ photos of my vacation to all my friends.

6. We can _____ into the hotel at 3:00.

7. Where can I _____ a plane ticket?

8. I always _____ photos of famous places I visit.

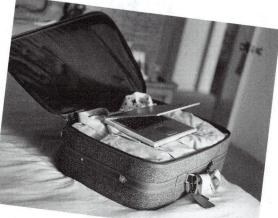

B Circle the correct answer.

1. This plane ticket is (my / mine).

2. Is this (him / his) car?

3. Please show this photo to (their / them).

4. This suitcase belongs to (her / hers).

5. These shopping bags are (our / ours).

6. Is this book (your / yours)?

C Complete the sentences with the correct pronoun form.

Example: These are their clothes.   These clothes are __*theirs*__ .

1. Is that my seat?   Is that _____?

2. Give her your passport.   Give your passport to _____.

3. These keys belong to him.   These are _____ keys.

4. Do these keys belong to you?   Are they _____ keys?

5. I talk to my parents a lot.   I talk to _____ every week.

2 Reading and Writing

A Read the article.

Travel Smart! ⓘ

Watch the weather!

Most people plan their vacations very carefully. They think a lot about plane tickets, passports, and hotel reservations. But they often forget about one important thing—the weather. You should learn about the right time to visit your vacation spot. Here is some information to help you plan your next vacation.

- **Italy** The weather is sunny all year, but it's sometimes cold in winter. April and May are warm and beautiful. From June to September, it's very hot.

- **Australia** Summer here is from December to April. It sometimes rains, but the weather is usually very good. In winter, it snows a little in some places, but most of Australia isn't very cold.

- **Hong Kong** The weather is hot and very humid here a lot of the year. In July and August, it's sometimes very windy, and there are bad storms. October and November are warm and not so humid, but in December and January, it gets very chilly sometimes.

- **Germany** From November to April, the weather is cold, cloudy, and snowy. In spring, it's warm, but there's a lot of rain. July and August are usually warm and sunny.

- **India** You shouldn't travel to India from June to September. There is a lot of rain everywhere. From November to April, after the rainy season, the weather is nice and cool. In April and May, it often gets very hot.

B Circle *T* for *true* and *F* for *false*.

1. T   F   In Germany, the weather is cool in spring.
2. T   F   It rains a lot in India in June.
3. T   F   It is never cold in Italy.
4. T   F   It is humid in Hong Kong in July.
5. T   F   It sometimes snows in Australia.
6. T   F   In Germany, it's rainy in July.

C For each place, write the best time for a vacation and the reason.

Place	Best Time	Why?
Italy		
Australia		
Hong Kong		
Germany		
India		

D Write a paragraph to someone who wants to visit your city. Tell the visitor what the weather is like and what they should bring.

_____
_____
_____
_____
_____
_____
_____
_____
_____
_____
_____
_____

1 Vocabulary Workout

A Circle the correct answer.

1. (Politicians / Physicians) give speeches.

2. (Doctors / Attorneys) help people stay healthy.

3. (Teenagers / Editors) are always less than 20 years old.

4. (Speakers / Directors) manage other workers.

5. (Musicians / Ambassadors) work for the government.

6. (Co-founders / Activists) run a company together.

B Which word is different? Cross out the word that doesn't fit.

1. doctor	teenager	physician
2. teacher	instructor	politician
3. co-founder	traveler	tourist
4. lawyer	attorney	ambassador
5. writer	explorer	editor

C Complete the sentences. Use words from Activity A. There may be more than one correct answer.

1. _____ need passports.

2. _____ change the words that people write.

3. _____ try to change the world.

4. _____ work in hospitals.

5. _____ know about the laws of a country.

2 Conversation Workout

A Read the sentences and agree or disagree. Use expressions from the box and give your reasons.

| Yeah, I agree. | Really? I don't think so. | Sorry, but I disagree. | I know. |

Example: **Your friend:** I think history is a boring subject.
You: _Really? I don't think so. I like to read about heroes._

1. **Your friend:** I think English is a difficult language.
   You: _____

2. **Your friend:** Bill Gates is a great hero.
   You: _____

3. **Your friend:** I think our city is a really boring place.
   You: _____

4. **Your friend:** Everything is very expensive in our country.
   You: _____

5. **Your friend:** Our teacher gives us too much homework!
   You: _____

B Number the sentences in order to make a conversation.

_____ Oskar Schindler in "Schindler's List."

_____ I'm writing a paper about a movie hero.

_____ Really? Why is he your choice?

_____ Well, he was very brave and he saved many people.

_____ That's interesting! Who are you writing about?

C Write the names of two movies about heroes.

1. _____   2. _____

Now write conversations about the movies.

1. **You:** _____
   Your friend: _____
   You: _____
   Your friend: _____
   You: _____

2. **You:** _____
   Your friend: _____
   You: _____
   Your friend: _____
   You: _____

3 Language Workout

A Complete the sentences with *was, were, in,* or *ago.*

1. Charlie Chaplin _____ born in London about 120 years _____.

2. His parents _____ singers.

3. Chaplin's films _____ usually very funny.

4. His first film _____ "Making a Living."

5. His movies _____ very popular for over 50 years.

6. Chaplin died in Switzerland _____ 1977.

B Make the sentences negative.

Example: My grandfather was famous.

*My grandfather was not famous.*_____

1. The Baker sisters were musicians.

   _____

2. Henry Ford was a politician.

   _____

3. The sky was clear last night.

   _____

4. The children were excited.

   _____

5. I was confused by the first question.

   _____

C Complete the conversations.

1. **A:** _____ Jenna in class yesterday?

   B: No, she _____. She _____ at home.

2. **A:** _____ Steve and Julia at the beach on Saturday?

   B: No, _____. They _____ at the library.

3. **A:** _____ Carlos at the pool last night?

   B: No, _____. He _____ in his office.

4. **A:** _____ your brother in Los Angeles last year?

   B: Yes, _____.

5. **A:** _____ Mr. and Mrs. Parks in California on vacation last week?

   B: No, _____. They _____ in Rome.

6. **A:** _____ you _____?

   B: No, _____. I _____.

Lesson B Personal heroes

1 Vocabulary and Language Workout

A Match the sentences. Write the letter of the answer on the line.

1. I went by myself. _____
2. I did it for myself. _____
3. I was good at it. _____
4. I needed to find someone. _____
5. I admired that woman. _____
6. I planned to do something fun. _____

a. I did it very well.
b. I looked forward to it.
c. I looked for her.
d. No one went with me.
e. I looked up to her.
f. I didn't do it for anyone else.

B Fill in the correct verb in the simple past tense. Pay attention to spelling.

| move | visit | study | stop | invite | try | hand | reply |

1. Mara _____ to my invitation right away.
2. Rolando _____ to call you, but you didn't answer your phone.
3. The teacher _____ us our test papers after class.
4. My uncle _____ to the city to get a better job.
5. We _____ a lot the night before the test.
6. I _____ Rosa to come to my party, but she was busy.
7. The rain _____ before morning.
8. Anna _____ her grandmother in the hospital yesterday.

C Write sentences about last night. Follow the example.

	Felipe	**Chris and Beth**	**Vera**	**you**
study	yes	no	no	
visit friends	no	yes	yes	
watch TV	no	no	yes	

Example: Felipe _studied last night. He didn't visit friends. He didn't watch TV._

1. Chris and Beth _____

_____

2. Vera_____

_____

3. I _____

_____

2 Reading and Writing

A Read the article.

Mother Teresa

A Hero for Our Time

Agnes Bojaxhiu was born in Yugoslavia in 1910. Her parents had a grocery store. As a child, she always wanted to help people. When she was 18, she went to Ireland to become a nun, and she changed her name to Mother Teresa. She traveled to India and worked as a teacher at a girls' high school for 17 years.

Then, in 1946, her life changed. She decided to take care of sick and dying people and to help the hungry and the homeless. She started a group for women who wanted to work with poor people. They opened a school for poor children in the city of Calcutta. Next, she started a home for people who were dying. For the next 50 years, Mother Teresa worked with poor people in many countries, like China, England, and Cuba.

In 1979, Mother Teresa received the Nobel Peace Prize. She was very famous, but she didn't change her simple life. She still lived with the poor people of Calcutta, and she still used all her time to help them.

Mother Teresa died on September 5, 1997, but her work continues. For many people around the world, she is a true hero, and they try to follow her example.

B Complete the chart about Mother Teresa with information from the reading.

Born	
Work	- teacher in a girl's school
How she became famous	
Died	

C Fill in the simple past tense of the verb.

Frida Kahlo is a hero to many people in Mexico. She (1. be) _____ born in Mexico in 1907.
She (2. be) _____ a great artist. She (3. marry) _____ Diego Rivera, another artist,
but they (4. have, not) _____ any children. She (5. paint) _____ many strange and
beautiful pictures, even though she (6. study, not) _____ art. She (7. use) _____
many ideas from Mexican culture in her paintings. She (8. be) _____ also very brave. After
a terrible accident in 1925, her health (9. be, not) _____ very good. But she (10. work)
_____ very hard and (11. create) _____ some of the most beautiful art in the world.

D Write about a hero in your country.

6 The Mind

Lesson A Try to remember!

1 Vocabulary Workout

A Match the sentence parts. Write the letter of the answer on the line.

1. Your memory is _____   a. your teacher is happy.

2. If you forget your mother's birthday, _____   b. stories of past experience.

3. If you remember your homework, _____   c. you forget things.

4. When your mind stops working, _____   d. she can't remember things easily.

5. Memories are _____   e. her 16th birthday.

6. When she is tired, _____   f. she feels sad.

7. She will never forget _____   g. the part of you that remembers.

B Answer the questions. Use the <u>underlined</u> word or phrase in your answer.

1. How do you <u>remember</u> important things?

_____

_____

2. What do you sometimes <u>forget</u>?

_____

_____

3. What things are most important for you to <u>remember</u> every day?

_____

_____

4. Describe one thing that you will never <u>forget</u>.

_____

_____

5. What is one of your best <u>memories</u>?

_____

_____

6. What did you <u>forget</u> to do in the past week?

_____

_____

7. Are you <u>good at remembering</u> things?

_____

_____

2 Conversation Workout

A   Write the expressions in the box in order from 'most sure' to 'least sure'.

I'm not sure.	Yes.	I have no idea.
I don't think so.	I think so.	Maybe.

How sure are you?

100%			0%
1. _Yes._	2. _____	4. _____	6. _____
	3. _____	5. _____	

B   A foreign visitor is asking questions about your city. Answer them using one of the expressions from the box.

1. Can I change money at the post office?
   _____
   _____

2. Are there any big department stores here?
   _____
   _____

3. Do they play baseball here?
   _____
   _____

4. Are taxis expensive here?
   _____
   _____

5. Is there a Japanese restaurant in this city?
   _____

6. Can I buy postcards of your city?
   _____

7. Are the hotels in your city clean?
   _____

8. Is there a train station in this city?
   _____

9. Is your airport very crowded?
   _____

10. Is there a place to swim?
   _____

3 Language Workout

A Look at Karen's list from yesterday. What did she do? Follow the example.

Friday

go to the post office — *She didn't go to the post office.* _____

1. buy food for dinner ✓ _____

2. do my math homework ✓ _____

3. take my books to the library _____

4. get new shoes _____

5. see Mr. Sanchez ✓ _____

B Complete the chart.

Verb	Simple past	Verb	Simple past
1. _____	ate	begin	13. _____
feel	2. _____	14. _____	won
forget	3. _____	drink	15. _____
come	4. _____	go	16. _____
5. _____	fell	17. _____	bought
speak	6. _____	teach	18. _____
bring	7. _____	give	19. _____
8. _____	got	20. _____	shook
9. _____	took	do	21. _____
make	10. _____	22. _____	said
know	11. _____	run	23. _____
12. _____	had	think	24. _____

C What did you do?

Yesterday

1. _____

2. _____

3. _____

Last week

1. _____

2. _____

3. _____

Last year

1. _____

2. _____

3. _____

Lesson B Go back to sleep!

1 Vocabulary and Language Workout

A Complete the paragraph. Use words from the box.

was asleep	get up	stayed up late	fall asleep
went to bed	woke me up	noon	midnight

I worked hard yesterday. Then I (1) _____
to study for a test. I finally (2) _____ at
(3) _____, but I didn't (4) _____
until 3:00 A.M. in the morning. It was strange, but I was too tired to
sleep. I (5) _____ when the alarm clock
(6) _____. That was at (7) _____.
But I didn't (8) _____ until almost 1:00.

B Find the mistake in each sentence and correct it.

1. Did you went to the movie last night with your friends?

   _____

2. Where do you go on vacation last year?

   _____

3. I remembered my sunglasses, but I didn't remembered my watch.

   _____

4. Yesterday I got up early, eat toast for breakfast, and went to school early.

   _____

5. What Julio did buy at the bookstore?

   _____

C Complete the conversation with questions.

Rick: I did something interesting last night.

Ellen: Really? What (1) _____?

Rick: I went to a new restaurant.

Ellen: Oh? (2) _____?

Rick: A new Japanese restaurant called Sakura.

Ellen: (3) _____?

Rick: We had fish.

Ellen: (4) _____?

Rick: Yes, I liked it a lot. It was delicious.

Ellen: (5) _____ Japanese beer?

Rick: No, I didn't. I drank tea.

2 Reading and Writing

A Read this website.

Sleep and Dreams

Brain waves during sleep

Scientists know that the brain is very active when a person is sleeping. There are five stages, or parts, of sleep, Stage 1 starts after you fall asleep. If there is a noise or a bright light, you wake up very easily. In Stage 2, your brain waves are very slow. Stage 3 and Stage 4 are deep sleep. It's very difficult to wake up then. Your body rests and grows during these stages.

Stage 5 is when you dream. Your eyes move a lot, and your brain waves are fast. This stage of sleep is very important for your memory. After Stage 5, you wake up a little, and then Stage 1 starts again. We go through the five stages of sleep four or five times every night, so we have many dreams in one night.

How much sleep do you need? The answer depends on your age. Babies should sleep fifteen to sixteen hours every day. Children and teenagers need nine or ten hours of sleep, but older people only need six to eight hours. If you sleep for only four hours one night, you may just feel tired the next day. But many nights of bad sleep can be bad for your health. People who don't get enough sleep get sick more often. And sleep is very important for learning. It's one reason why students should go to bed early!

B Answer the questions.

1. How many stages of sleep are there? _____

2. When do people dream? _____

3. How many times do we have Stage 1 every night? _____

4. When does your body grow? _____

5. How much sleep do babies need? _____

6. Why should students sleep a lot? _____

7. Look at the last paragraph again. How much sleep should you get? _____

8. Do you get enough sleep? _____

C Complete the conversation with the correct simple past tense forms.

A: When (1. I/be) _____ ten years old, my family went on vacation.

B: Where (2. you/go) _____?

A: Florida!

B: (3. you/enjoy) _____ yourself?

A: Yes, I did. It was fun!

B: How many days (4. you/stay) _____ there?

A: (5. we/stay) _____ for three days. (6. we/go) _____ to the beach and (7. we/win) _____ some prizes at the games.

B: Do you want to go back again?

A: Sure! (8. I/have) _____ a great time.

D Write about a happy memory from when you were a child.

_____

_____

_____

_____

_____

_____

_____

_____

_____

_____

_____

_____

_____

_____

_____

_____

_____

7 In the City

Lesson A Places in my neighborhood

1 Vocabulary Workout

A Match the words that go together. Write the letter of the answer on the line.

1. train _____   a. salon
2. nail _____   b. club
3. taxi _____   c. store
4. grocery _____   d. station
5. health _____   e. shop
6. copy _____   f. stand

B Solve this crossword puzzle.

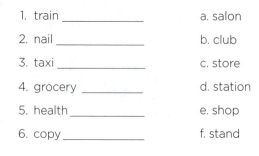

Down

1. You exercise there.
3. You see films there. It's a movie _____.
4. You buy books there.
5. They're two words that mean "exercise."
6. If you miss breakfast, you _____ it.

Across

2. You can get money from it.
7. It's like a cafe.
8. It's a very small place that sells things.
9. You can dance there.

   It's a night _____.
10. You can change how you look there.

    It's a _____ salon.

2 Conversation Workout

A Unscramble the sentences.

1. right / straight / go / and / turn

   _____

2. Main / on / left / Street / turn

   _____

3. on / it's / First Avenue / the / of / corner / Court Street / and

   _____

4. block / of / it's / in / middle / the / the

   _____

5. left / go / one / and / block / turn

   _____

B Look at the map and complete the conversations.

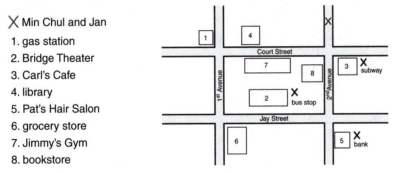

✗ Min Chul and Jan
1. gas station
2. Bridge Theater
3. Carl's Cafe
4. library
5. Pat's Hair Salon
6. grocery store
7. Jimmy's Gym
8. bookstore

Example: **A:** Is there a coffee shop around here?

B: Yes. There's a cafe on <u>*the corner of Court Street and 2ⁿᵈ Avenue.*</u> _____.

1. **A:** Excuse me. Where's the grocery store?

   B: It's on the _____.

2. **A:** Where's Jimmy's Gym?

   B: It's on _____. It's in the middle _____.

3. **A:** Is there a movie theater near here?

   B: Yes. The Bridge Theater is on _____. It's _____ the bus stop.

4. **A:** What is that building on Court Street across from Jimmy's Gym?

   B: That's the _____.

C Now write conversations about your neighborhood.

Visitor: Excuse me. Is there a coffee shop near here?

You: _____

Visitor: And is there a bank or an ATM?

You: _____

3 Language Workout

A Look at the map. Answer the questions. Use the prepositions in parentheses.

Example: Where is the post office? (on) *It's on Park Avenue.*_____

1. Where is the supermarket? (on) _____

2. Where is the drugstore? (across) _____

   _____

3. Where is the movie theater? (on, next to) _____

   _____

4. Where is the Modern Language Institute? (on) _____

5. Where is the bank? (corner) _____

6. Where is the Post Office? (across) _____

7. Where is the bus stop? (next to) _____

B Write two sentences for each place. Use *near, across from, next to, in front of, behind,* or *between.*

1. Where is your house?

   _____

   _____

2. Where is your school?

   _____

   _____

3. Where is your favorite restaurant?

   _____

   _____

4. Where is your best friend's house?

   _____

   _____

Lesson B Cities around the world

1 Vocabulary and Language Workout

A Complete the sentences with the words from the box.

stuck	weather	population	pollution
traffic	form	transportation	affordable

1. My country has a small _____. Only two million people live here.

2. The _____ in Hawaii is very good. It's always warm and sunny.

3. It's easy to drive through my neighborhood. I never get _____ in traffic.

4. _____ is a big problem in London. The streets are small and there are a lot of cars.

5. Everything is expensive in my city. It isn't a very _____ place.

6. There is a lot of _____ . The air and water are very dirty.

7. Buses and subways are two kinds of _____ .

8. My bicycle is my favorite _____ of transportation.

B Are these things good or bad for a city? Write them in the correct box. Add two more things.

very little pollution	bad weather	a very large population
affordable prices	a lot of public transportation	_____
a lot of traffic	severe winters	_____

Good Things	Bad Things

C Complete the questions with *How much* or *How many.* Then write the answers.

1. _____ people are there in your city?

   _____

2. _____ traffic is there?

   _____

3. _____ pollution is there?

   _____

4. _____ parks are there?

   _____

5. _____ public transportation is there?

   _____

6. _____ good restaurants are there?

   _____

2 Reading and Writing

A Read the magazine article.

🌐🔍 TRAVEL GUIDE:

Choosing a City

Istanbul, Turkey

Istanbul is a very unusual city—one part is in Europe, and the other part is in Asia. About 9 million people live there. Visitors love Istanbul because it has many beautiful, old buildings, and the food is great. At night, the seafood restaurants are very popular. And everything in Istanbul is very affordable for visitors. Traffic is a problem in the city, because there are too many cars for the old streets. There are also subways, trains, and buses, and some people take boats to go between the European side and the Asian side. The weather is very good in summer, but in winter it's sometimes very cold.

Vancouver, Canada

Vancouver is one of the most beautiful cities in the world. It's near the mountains and the sea, and there are many great parks where you can walk, ride a bicycle, or just relax. The city has good public transportation, with buses and fast trains that go everywhere. There are about 600,000 people in Vancouver, but it's a very clean city, and there's not much pollution. Two bad points—prices there are very high, and the weather is not very good. Vancouver is famous for rain! But there are many good museums for those rainy days, and in the evening, the city has great restaurants and nightclubs to visit.

B Find information about the two cities and write it in the chart.

	Istanbul	Vancouver
Location		
Population		
Weather		
Transportation		
Affordability		

C Read the paragraph. Find eight spelling mistakes and correct them.

Singapore is a great city for a vacation. There are alot of interesting things to see. You can visit Chinatown and Little India, and go shopping on Orchard Road. Singapore also has many good restarants. There are some great beaches for swimming naer the city, and the parks are really beutiful. The city has very good public transportion. You can take a bus, trane or subway. It's a safe city. It's also a clean city. There isn't much polution. The only problem is that Singapore is expensiev.

D Write about a city you think is good for a vacation.

8 All About You

Lesson A Fun activities

1 Vocabulary Workout

A Unscramble the names of these fun activities.

1. g o a y   _____
2. s n i t n e   _____
3. a a b b l l e s _____
4. c r e s o c   _____
5. s l a t i p e   _____
6. b m n n a i t d o _____
7. d o u j   _____
8. c r a b e o i s _____

B Write the words from exercise A in the boxes. Add other fun activities to the boxes.

I like it. 🙂	It's OK. 😐	I don't like it. 🙁

C Complete the sentences with *play, do* or *go*. Remember to use the correct verb form.

1. Ramon and Felipe _____ soccer every Saturday.

2. It's cold so we can't _____ swimming at the beach.

3. Eun-Mi _____ basketball for her school team.

4. Do you _____ tennis in the park?

5. People usually _____ yoga indoors.

6. John _____ bowling with his friends every week.

7. I have a tent. Let's _____ camping.

8. I usually _____ Pilates on Monday nights.

2　Conversation Workout

A　Unscramble the sentences to make conversations.

1. **Andy:** soccer / do / play / want / you / to

   _____

   Jeff: I'd / love / sure / to

   _____

2. **Maria:** some / want / you / do / water / more

   _____

   Anna: thanks / I'm / fine / no　　(Make two sentences.)

   _____

3. **David:** come / you / do / to / want

   _____

   Alan: sorry / busy / can't / I'm / I　(Make two sentences.)

   _____

B　Now write new conversations.

1. swimming / tomorrow / pool / in Center Park

   You: _____

   Your friend: _____

   You: _____

   Your friend: Sure, _____

2. baseball / tonight / a big test tomorrow

   You: _____

   Your friend: _____

   You: _____

   Your friend: Sorry, _____

3. (your ideas)

   You: _____

   Your friend: _____

   You: _____

   Your friend: Sure, _____

4. (your ideas)

   You: _____

   Your friend: _____

   You: _____

   Your friend: Sorry, _____

3 Language Workout

A Choose the correct words to complete each sentence.

1. **Rita:** Do you plan _____ tennis lessons?

   a. take   b. to take

   Ali: Yes, I like _____.

   a. play tennis   b. to play tennis

2. **Ali:** Do you often _____?

   a. go to bowling   b. go bowling

   Rita: Oh, yes. I love _____.

   a. bowling   b. go bowling

3. **Ali:** I expect _____.

   a. to play basketball tonight
   b. playing basketball tonight

   Rita: I hate _____.

   a. play basketball   b. basketball

4. **Rita:** Do you want _____?

   a. some ice cream   b. have some
   ice cream

   Ali: No, thanks. I don't like _____ just before
   I go running.

   a. to eat   b. eat

5. **Ali:** How did you learn _____?

   a. playing   b. to play

   Rita: I loved _____ games and I learned it that way.

   a. watching volleyball   b. watch volleyball

B Rewrite the sentences. Correct one mistake in each sentence.

1. I expect winning the game tonight.

   _____

2. Where did you learn play tennis?

   _____

3. She enjoys to go swimming.

   _____

4. They plan do yoga this evening.

   _____

1 Vocabulary and Language Workout

A Complete the words for personal qualities.

1. Selma is really a __ __ __ __ __ __ s. She wants to be president someday.

2. Artists are usually very c __ __ __ __ __ __ __. They have lots of original ideas.

3. Are you o __ __ __ __ __ __ __? Do you have a special place to put everything?

4. Jared is very s __ __ __ __ __ __. He doesn't spend money on other people.

5. I __ __ __ __ __ __ __ people do things without thinking.

6. My children are very b __ __ __ __ __. They get good grades in school.

7. Athletes are often very c __ __ __ __ __ __ __ __ __. They try hard to win.

8. She is a very p __ __ __ __ __ person. She doesn't talk about herself very much.

B Write descriptions of two friends. Write about their personalities and give examples.

1. Name: _____ Description: _____

_____

_____

_____

2. Name: _____ Description: _____

_____

_____

_____

C Write these time expressions in order of frequency. Then write a sentence for each one.

| every day | every Sunday | four times a year | hardly ever |
| twice a month | once in a while | all the time | never |

Example: all the time *I wear glasses all the time.* _____

1. _____ _____

2. _____ _____

3. _____ _____

4. _____ _____

5. _____ _____

6. _____ _____

7. _____ _____

2 Reading and Writing

A Read the article.

The Right Personality

Do you have the right personality for these jobs? We asked some famous people what it takes to be a success in their field.

Don Pierce, star of the movie *Race Against Time*

A good actor wants very much to succeed. Most laid back actors never become famous. Successful actors also get to know the right people in Hollywood. In addition, they are able to think creatively. And they understand people very well. That helps them understand the different characters they play on stage and in the movies.

Dr. Janice Wong, author of *Perfect Health Now*

The most important thing for a good doctor is being a good listener. You have to understand people and their problems. A good doctor likes to solve problems and always wants to help his or her patients. And you can't be impulsive—you should always be careful. Sometimes the first answer you think of isn't the right answer.

Daniel Vasquez, president of Interex Corporation

To be a success in business, you have to work well with groups of people. At the same time, you need to have strong opinions and be able to explain your opinions clearly. Good businesspeople are able to make quick decisions and try new ideas. They are very organized and they work very long hours.

B In the article, which things are important for each job?

	actor	doctor	businessperson
1. good listener		X	
2. ambitious			
3. impulsive			
4. creative			
5. understand people			
6. careful			
7. have strong opinions			
8. want to help people			
9. organized			
10. work well with people			

C Read and complete the paragraph. Use the words from the box.

generous   organized   competitive   patient   private

A good athlete is (1.)_____. He or she must really want to win! Athletes must also be (2.)_____ during training sessions. Progress doesn't always come quickly. Being (3.)_____ is also important. There's nothing worse than a player who can't find his equipment. Although most athletes are quite talkative, some of them have a (4.)_____ side as well. They don't want everyone to know everything about them. The best athletes are also (5.)_____. They help their team members score points; they don't try to score all the points themselves.

D What makes a good teacher? Write a paragraph with your ideas.

_____

_____

_____

_____

_____

_____

_____

_____

9 Change

Lesson A I need a change

1 Vocabulary Workout

A Match the sentence halves that go together. Write the letter of the answer on the line.

1. Ellen wants to quit _____   a. in good shape.

2. Bill wants to be _____   b. job.

3. Ming doesn't want to gain _____   c. out of shape.

4. Maria wants to find _____   d. smoking.

5. Ali lost his _____   e. less money.

6. Sandra wants to make _____   f. a better job.

7. Tony doesn't want to be _____   g. weight.

8. I don't want to earn _____   h. more money.

B Read the first sentence. Write a second sentence. Follow the example. Use words from this unit or add your own ideas.

Example: I make only $4.00 an hour.   *I want to earn more money.* _____

1. I weigh 150 kilos. _____

2. I smoke too much. _____

3. I am not in good shape. _____

4. I don't have a job. _____

5. I am too thin. _____

6. I am tired all the time. _____

C What do you want to change about your life? Write five sentences. Follow the example:

Example: *I want to get a new job.* _____

1. _____

2. _____

3. _____

4. _____

5. _____

2 Conversation Workout

A Use the sentences in the box to make a conversation.

> Thanks a lot!
>
> Oh no! I don't have my English book.
>
> Yes, I have English class at 10:00. Can I borrow yours?
>
> Sure, no problem.
>
> Do you need it today?

Tomas: _____

_____

Klara: _____

_____

Tomas: _____

_____

Klara: _____

_____

Tomas: _____

_____

B Use the words to make questions and answers.

Example: ? / borrow / I / your / can / dictionary   _Can I borrow your dictionary?_

1. . / go / you / sure / here / ,

_____

2. ? / lend / could / me / you / five dollars

_____

3. ? / OK / it / is / use / pen / your / if / I

_____

4. ? / please / you / would / me / lend / a dollar

_____

5. . / need / I / get / to / a haircut

_____

C Now write new conversations making and responding to requests.

1. cell phone / call my mother

Wendy: _____

Pam: _____

Wendy: _____

Pam: _____

Wendy: _____

2. (your idea)

Your friend: _____

You: _____

Your friend: _____

You: _____

Your friend: _____

3 Language Workout

A Write what each person likes to do and what they would like to do.

1. Tim / use computers, be a programmer

   Tim likes to use computers. He'd like to be a programmer.

2. Barbara / draw, make beautiful clothes

   _____

3. Jose Luis / travel, practice his English

   _____

4. Katie / talk to people, work in a restaurant

   _____

5. you / ?

   _____

B Fill in the spaces with *like to* or *would like to*.

1. We always go to New York on vacation. Next year, I _____ go to Miami.

2. When I get up, I always _____ drink coffee and read the newspaper.

3. Myoung-Hee _____ study English in Canada this summer.

4. Jeff _____ have a big dog, but he lives in a very small apartment.

5. I _____ visit my grandmother every Sunday because she always cooks a big dinner for me.

6. Francisco doesn't like his work. He _____ get a new job.

C Answer the questions with your own information.

1. What do you like to do in the evening?

   _____

2. What would you like to do this evening?

   _____

3. What do you like to do on vacation?

   _____

4. What would you like to do on your next vacation?

   _____

5. What do you like to do in English class?

   _____

6. What would you like to do next time in English class?

   _____

Lesson B Plans and dreams

1 Vocabulary and Language Workout

A Complete each sentence with the correct word or phrase from the box.

take off	take	get	apply for
take it	become	about to	get ready

1. I want to _____ a job as soon as I finish school.

2. I'd like to _____ a doctor.

3. I am _____ take my final exams.

4. The English exam will _____ three hours.

5. I have to go and _____ for the exam right now.

6. After my exams, I will _____ two weeks and just relax.

7. Then I will _____ easy for a while.

8. After that, I will _____ a job. I hope I get one soon!

B Write answers about future plans.

	Rachel	Ken	Dan and Carol	You
move to another city	no	yes	no	
travel	yes	no	yes	
start a business	yes	no	no	

1. What is Rachel going to do in the future? _She isn't going to move to another city. She is going to travel and start a business._
_____

2. What is Ken going to do in the future? _____
_____

3. What are Dan and Carol going to do in the future? _____
_____

4. What are you going to do in the future?_____
_____

C Answer the questions with your own information.

1. What is one of your dreams for the future? _____
_____

2. Would you like to get married soon? Why or why not? _____
_____

3. Would you like to become a teacher? Why or why not? _____
_____

2 Reading and Writing

A Read the article.

Find Your Dream
by Sandra Bolen

1. _____

We all have dreams, but some people actually make their dreams come true. Their secret? They quit dreaming, and they start doing. Even a very big dream starts with small steps, and small goals.

2. _____

Maybe your dream is to become a doctor. Start by thinking about small goals for your self. Ask, "What can I do today?" You can't start medical school today, but you can send e-mails and make phone calls to get information about medical schools. Make a list of schools to call, and then call a few of them every day.

3. _____

Another good idea is talking to people who are doing your dream job. Do you dream about having your own restaurant? Go to your favorite restaurant and ask the owner lots of questions. Most people like to talk about their work.

4. _____

What do you need for your dream? Tell friends and family members—many of them can help you. For example, you want to become an artist. You need a lot of cheap paper for drawing. Maybe your friend's brother throws away a lot of big paper at his office. So, share your dream with the world!

B Write the correct title for each section of the article.

Start Today

Ask for Help

Learn from Other People

From Dream to Real Life

C The underlined words in this paragraph are incorrect. Write the correct words above the incorrect ones. Use words from this unit.

      become
I plan to (1.) ~~apply for~~ a doctor. I studied for eight years. Now I am (2.) <u>taking ready</u> to work. But first,

I need to (3.) <u>take some time it</u> for a vacation. For three weeks I plan to just (4.) <u>get it</u> easy. Then I will start

(5.) <u>applying off</u> jobs. Right now I am (6.) <u>about for</u> leave for the airport. My plane (7.) <u>gets off</u> at 2:00!

D Write about how to be a successful language learner. Use your own ideas.

1 Vocabulary Workout

A Unscramble the words for parts of the body.

1. d a n h _____
2. t s e h c _____
3. m a r _____
4. t o f o _____
5. k n e c _____
6. d e a h _____
7. h s u d l o r e _____
8. g e l _____

B Write the words in the correct order.

1. hand, neck, shoulder, arm

the top part	lower	still lower	the lowest part

2. foot, head, chest, leg

the top part	lower	still lower	the lowest part

C Complete the sentences with words from the box. Use plural forms when necessary.

stomach	foot	short	narrow	bone	skin	muscle	hand	long	strong

1. I put my left shoe on my left _____.
2. I have strong _____ in my arms.
3. Inside the legs are long, hard _____.
4. The _____ covers the outside of the body.
5. When you eat, your _____ gets full.
6. Your _____ is at the end of your arm.
7. You can't carry a lot of things if you have _____ arms.
8. A swimmer must have very _____ arms.
9. A man has broad shoulders, but a boy has _____ ones.
10. People with _____ legs can run faster than people with short legs.

2 Conversation Workout

A Write the sentences in the correct order to make a conversation.

What's wrong?

I have a headache and I feel really tired.

Really? Why not?

Oh, sorry to hear that. Get some rest and I'll call you in the morning.

I don't feel well.

I can't meet you tonight.

Mario: Sorry, but _____

Tina: _____

Mario: _____

Tina: _____

Mario: _____

Tina: _____

B Now write three new conversations. Give your own advice.

1. (sore throat / can't talk)

Carla: _____

Jan: _____

Carla: _____

Jan: _____

Carla: _____

Jan: _____

2. (fever / feel really hot)

Maria: _____

Jim: _____

Maria: _____

Jim: _____

Maria: _____

Jim: _____

3. (your own idea)

Martin: _____

Judy: _____

Martin: _____

Judy: _____

Martin: _____

Judy: _____

3 Language Workout

A A mother is talking to her children. Write sentences with imperatives.

wash the dishes—yes	clean the table—yes	eat all the ice cream—no
call your friends—no	watch TV now—no	put away the dishes—yes
take out the garbage—yes	play with the dog—no	

This kitchen looks terrible. *Wash the dishes.*

_____

_____

_____

B Write advice for these people. Use imperatives.

1. I love coffee, but I can't sleep at night.

_____

2. My stomach hurts.

_____

3. I have a very bad sore throat.

_____

4. I'm a teacher. My feet hurt after work every day.

_____

5. I have a terrible cough.

_____

6. I want to quit smoking.

_____

C Circle the correct word or words.

1. Please bring me (a glass / a cup) of hot coffee.

2. Can I have (a glass / a piece) of cake?

3. After lunch I drank (a glass / a piece) of milk.

4. I sometimes put (a cup / a bit) of salt on my food.

Lesson B Energy and stress

1 Vocabulary and Language Workout

A Complete the sentences with words from the box.

stressed	pressure	unhealthy	reduce
energy	energetic	lucky	

1. Martha has six children and two part-time jobs. She is under a lot of _____.

2. I didn't study for my test, but I still got 100. I guess I'm really _____.

3. Get some exercise every day and go to bed early. You'll have more _____.

4. Mr. Kwan feels _____. His plane is late and he has an important meeting in two hours.

5. To make more time for exercise, you should _____ your hours of TV watching.

6. My sister is very _____. She gets up at 6:00 every day and goes swimming before work.

7. Alex is a very _____ person. He has colds and fevers all the time.

B Write sentences with *when*. Follow the examples.

Examples: have a cold / sleep a lot   *When I have a cold, I sleep a lot.*

feel nervous / drink coffee   *I feel nervous when I drink coffee.*

1. study for six hours / feel exhausted

_____

2. talk to my friend Anna / have a problem

_____

3. go on vacation / sleep very late

_____

4. feel healthy / exercise every day

_____

5. take aspirin / have a headache

_____

C Complete the sentences with your own ideas.

1. When I have a test, _____

2. When I get up very early, _____

3. When I feel stressed, _____

4. When I have free time, _____

5. When I have a lot of energy, _____

2 Reading and Writing

A   Read the article.

Home Remedies
by Grandma Mabel

A long time ago, when people were sick, they didn't go to the doctor, and they didn't buy medicine from the drugstore. Instead, they used home remedies—medicine made from things at home. Today, many people like to use home remedies because they are cheap and easy to use. Here are some old home remedies from the United States.

- Don't eat dinner late at night. Have a small, light dinner early in the evening.
- Eat lettuce for dinner. It helps you feel calm.
- Eat raw onions to help you sleep.

- Cook an onion and put the hot onion on your ear.
- Put some salt in a bag, heat the bag, and put it on the side of your head.
- Put warm oil in your ear.

- Don't eat very cold food, like ice cream.
- Lie down and close your eyes. Breathe calmly, and don't think about anything.
- Put a hot cloth on your head, above your eyes.

- Eat a lot of yogurt to help your stomach work better.
- Drink tea made from the ginger, peppermint, or chamomile plants.
- Reduce alcohol, tea, and coffee.

B   Write the correct title for each section. Use four of the titles.

When you have a headache   When your ear hurts

When your feet hurt   When you have sleep problems

When you have stomach problems

C Fill in the spaces with the correct imperative form.

cook	take	put	don't	stay	drink	go

We have many home remedies for coughs in my country. When you have a cough, (1.)_____ a very hot bath. (2.)_____ tea with a lot of sugar. (3.)_____ exercise because that makes coughs worse. (4.)_____ warm and (5.)_____ to bed if the weather is cold. (6.)_____ some eggs and (7.)_____ them on your chest. My grandmother always uses these home remedies.

D Write about home remedies for colds in your country.

_____

_____

_____

_____

_____

_____

_____

_____

_____

_____

_____

_____

_____

_____

_____

That's Amazing

Lesson A Terrific talents

1 Vocabulary Workout

A Unscramble the words.

1. b a i i l y t   a _ _ _ _ _ _ _
2. a n a t r u l   n _ _ _ _ _ _ _
3. t l e n a t   t _ _ _ _ _ _
4. s h e r a c   s _ _ _ _ _ _

5. i t h s   h _ _ _
6. s d v i o e   v _ _ _ _ _ _
7. t o u s c   s _ _ _ _ _
8. t o p s   p _ _ _ _

B Match each sentence starter with the correct ending.

1. Did your post get any _____   a. scout?
2. When did he post the _____   b. abilities?
3. Does he have any acting _____   c. show?
4. Does she have several other _____   d. post?
5. How many photos did you _____   e. talent?
6. Did you know she was so _____   f. hits?
7. Is he a talent _____   g. talented?
8. Did she perform in a talent _____   h. video?

C Use the cue words to write questions. Then answer the questions. Use your own ideas.

Example: **Q:** she / talent   _Does she have any talent?_

          A: (your idea)   _Yes. She plays the piano._

1. **Q:** he / natural ability   _____

   A: _____

2. **Q:** the site / get / many hits   _____

   A: _____

3. **Q:** they / good at   _____

   A: _____

4. **Q:** he / give up   _____

   A: _____

5. **Q:** she / talent scout   _____

   A: _____

2 Conversation Workout

A Unscramble the words to make compliments.

1. nice / a / that's / car

_____

2. great / what / a / meal

_____

3. dance / can / really / you / well

_____

4. like / your / shoes / a lot / I

_____

5. wonderful / a / story / that's

_____

B Write compliments for these situations.

1. Your friend is wearing a new jacket.

_____

2. Your classmate is singing and it sounds great.

_____

3. Your friend cooks a delicious dinner for you.

_____

4. You see your neighbor's beautiful garden.

_____

5. Your sister paints a pretty picture.

_____

C Answer the compliments and add information.

Example: That's a great shirt.

Thanks, I got it at Metro Department Store.

1. Your dog is really cute.

_____

2. You speak English very well.

_____

3. Your role play was really funny.

_____

4. That's a cool T-shirt.

_____

3 Language Workout

A Write sentences about the information in the chart. Follow the example.

	swim	cook	speak English
Yoshi, age ten	yes	no	no
Yoshi, now	yes	yes	no
Estela, age ten	no	no	no
Estela, now	yes	no	yes
You, age ten			
You, now			

Yoshi

He *could swim when he was ten.*   He *can swim now.*

1. He _____ cook when he was ten.   He _____ now.

2. He _____ when he was ten.   He _____ now.

Estela

3. She _____.   She _____ now.

4. She _____.   She _____ now.

5. She _____.   She _____ now.

You

6. I _____.   I _____ now.

7. I _____.   I _____ now.

8. I _____.   I _____ now.

B Rewrite the sentences. Use the correct form of *know how to* in place of *can, can't, could* and *couldn't.*

1. He can't speak French.

_____

2. She couldn't swim when she was two.

_____

3. She can make music videos.

_____

4. He could walk when he was seven months old.

_____

Lesson B A sense of achievement

1 Vocabulary and Language Workout

A Match each sentence starter with the correct ending.

1. A <u>gambler</u> is always _____
2. I'm going to <u>play it safe</u> and take _____
3. I hope to <u>have a chance</u> _____
4. I plan to reach _____
5. A <u>curious</u> person wants to know _____
6. They have a chance of _____
7. An <u>ambitious</u> person wants to be _____
8. A <u>famous</u> person is known by _____

a. to visit Paris someday.
b. a big success.
c. this <u>goal</u> by age 35.
d. a risk-taker.
e. everyone.
f. my umbrella.
g. all the answers.
h. winning <u>first</u> prize.

B Look back at the underlined words in activity A. Put them in the correct box.

Noun	Verb	Adjective

C Rewrite the sentences. Change the word *so* to *because*, or change the word *because* to *so*.

Example: Karen can't drive because she is only 12 years old.

   Karen is only 12 years old so she can't drive.

1. I was tired so I went to bed.

   _____

2. They bought the car because it was cheap.

   _____

3. The test is tomorrow so we should study now.

   _____

4. I will leave early because I don't want to be late.

   _____

5. The movie was boring so I left.

   _____

2 Reading and Writing

A Read this web site.

About Us   **Programs**   **Get Involved**   **Contact Us**

Amazing Musicians: Adam Ho

Adam Ho is an amazing musician. He plays the electric guitar, sings, writes his own music, and records music in his own home studio. He plays at concerts all around California, and performs music for TV commercials. An article about him was on the front page of a Los Angeles newspaper. Well, what's unusual about that?

Adam is 14 years old. He was only 12 when his story and photo appeared in the newspaper! He has received many prizes for his musical talent. When he was nine, he won first prize in a music contest. In 2009, he received an award for a TV commercial he made. When he appeared on a national TV talent show, he won first prize with the best score possible.

Adam has other talents and interests, too. He enjoys swimming, tennis, martial arts, and acting. But mostly he loves to play the guitar. He often plays on a shopping street in Santa Monica, California. People stop to listen and give him money—and maybe buy one of his CDs.

Adam wants to play more concerts, and he gives guitar lessons for beginners. His advice for other young musicians: "I practice almost two hours a day for better technique and playing. All you have to do is be patient, and you'll make it."

B Circle the letter of the correct answer.

1. Adam is amazing because he is very _____.

   a. fast   b. strong   c. young

2. He won a music contest when he was _____.

   a. nine   b. twelve   c. fourteen

3. Adam also likes _____.

   a. sports   b. chess   c. animals

4. He _____ other guitar players.

   a. teaches   b. plays with   c. takes lessons with

5. Adam _____ to earn money.

   a. sells newspapers   b. takes photos   c. sells CDs

C Find the eight spelling mistakes and correct them.

When I was a high school student, I wanted to go on a school trip. My parents said it was too expencive for my family, so I decided to earn the mony myself. I got a part-time job in a grocery store. The work was very dificult, and I got really tiered, but I didn't give up. I worked every Friday and Saterday night for a whole year. I saved everything I earned, and at the end of the yaer, I had enough money. I had a great time on the school trip, and my hard work at the grocery store made it posible. For me, it was a big acheivement.

D Write about a big achievement by you or another person.

_____
_____
_____
_____
_____
_____
_____
_____
_____
_____
_____
_____
_____

12 At the Movies

Lesson A Now showing at a theater near you

1 Vocabulary Workout

A Complete the sentences with words from the box.

| action | classics | horror | science fiction | musical | romantic comedies |

1. People usually fall in love in _____.
2. Many _____ movies are all about the future.
3. Good old movies are often called _____.
4. A movie with a lot of singing and dancing is a _____.
5. _____ movies often have car chases and gun fights.
6. Movies that scare people are called _____ movies.

B Unscramble the words to make sentences.

1. movies / into / I'm / action / not

_____

2. always / ending / like / a / I / happy

_____

3. good / feel / make / romantic / me / comedies

_____

4. crazy / musicals / she's / about / not

_____

5. movies / like / scary / don't / I

_____

6. classic / fan / he's / movies / a / of / big

_____

C Complete the chart.

A movie I liked

name of the movie	kind of movie	actors

A movie I didn't like

name of the movie	kind of movie	actors

2 Conversation Workout

A Complete the conversation with words from the box. Pay attention to capital letters.

take	tell	there	this	hang	thanks	please	sorry	here	calling

Larry: Hello?

Mina: Hi, is Beth (1.)_____, (2.)_____?

Larry: Who's (3.)_____?

Mina: (4.)_____ is Mina, a friend from school.

Larry: OK. (5.)_____ on a minute.

Mina: (6.)_____.

Larry: *(a few seconds later)* Hello? (7.)_____, Beth's not (8.)_____.
Can I (9.)_____ a message?

Mina: Yeah. There's a party on Friday at John's house. It's at 8:00.

Larry: OK. I'll (10.)_____ her.

Mina: Thanks a lot.

B Now write new conversations.

1. You have two tickets to a concert. Decide what kind of concert, and what time. Call your classmate, Carlos. His mother answers the phone.

Mother: Hello?

You: _____

Mother: _____

You: _____

Mother: _____

You: _____

Mother: *(a few seconds later)* _____

You: _____

Mother: _____

You: _____

2. You have two tickets to a movie. Decide what kind of movie, and what time. Call your friend, Judy. Her sister answers the phone.

Sister: Hello?

You: _____

Sister: _____

You: _____

Sister: _____

You: _____

Sister: *(a few seconds later)* _____

You: _____

Sister: _____

You: _____

3 Language Workout

A Complete the sentences with the *-ed* or *-ing* adjective.

1. (bore) I fell asleep during the movie.

    I was very _____.

    The movie was really _____.

2. (interest) Julia loves to read books about famous athletes.

    She thinks they are very _____.

    She's very _____ in famous athletes.

3. (disappoint) Our favorite baseball team lost the game.

    It was a very _____ game.

    We were really _____ in our team.

4. (excite) My brother won the music contest!

    That was _____ news.

    My family was very _____.

5. (confuse) Math is a difficult subject for David.

    It is very _____ for him.

    He often gets _____ in class.

6. (exhaust) I just finished working 12 hours straight.

    It was an _____ day for me.

    I am totally _____.

7. (shock) I saw a horror movie on TV last night.

    The story was really _____.

    I was _____ at the end of the movie.

B Complete the sentences with the correct adjective form of a word from the box.

interest   bore   excite   confuse   disappoint   shock

1. That movie was too _____. I couldn't understand the story.

2. I do the same thing every day at work. My job is really _____.

3. I was _____ when I heard the terrible news.

4. Are you _____ in old movies?

5. Chris was _____ with his low score on the exam.

6. Action movies are very _____. They make me want to jump up out of my seat.

C Now write sentences. Use your own ideas.

1. (boring) _____

2. (excited) _____

3. (confusing) _____

4. (exhausted) _____

5. (interesting) _____

Lesson B On the set

1 Vocabulary and Language Workout

A Complete the paragraph with words from the box.

| sit around | screen | festivals | directors | stars | theater | extras | shooting |

So you want to be in the movies...

Everyone thinks that (1.)_____ a movie is exciting and fun. Movie
(2.)_____ seem to have such wonderful lives. However, there are a
lot of things that you don't see on the (3.)_____. Many actors work
as (4.)_____ for years before they get a starring role. The actors
sometimes get really bored. They have to (5.)_____ for hours waiting.
And some (6.)_____ can be difficult to work with. Actors also have
to go to film (7.)_____ and talk about the movies they have made.
It takes a lot of time. So the next time you go to a movie (8.)_____,
you should realize that the life of a movie star up on screen isn't always so
much fun.

B Write questions and answers about weekend plans. Use the present continuous as future.

	Jeff	Maki	Matt and Angie	you
Saturday	go to the beach	clean her apartment	go shopping	
Sunday	see a movie with his brother	study for a science exam	cook a big dinner	

1. What's Jeff doing on Saturday?   He's going to the beach.

_____ on Sunday?   _____

2. (Maki) _____

_____

3. (Matt and Angie) _____

_____

4. (you) _____

_____

2 Reading and Writing

A Read the movie listings.

In Theaters This Week

1. The Blackest Night _____
In this new science fiction film, Brandon Carter and
Leslie Kim star as two astronauts who have a terrible
accident. They are trapped on the dark side of the
Moon, with just a little food, air, and water. Can they
survive? It's an exciting two hours!

2. Winter and Spring _____
This movie is about two medical students who fall in
love. They have big plans for the future—getting
married, having a baby, starting a hospital for poor
children. Then Paul (played by Matt Keene) gets very
sick, and Melissa (Jessica Mays) must make a difficult
decision. (Don't worry, the end is happy!)

3. My New Job _____
You can't believe the plot of this new comedy, but it's
very, very funny. A famous soccer star named Adriano
(played by Paulo Costa) gets a job teaching at a
kindergarten. The children do many crazy things, but
Adriano learns some very important lessons from a little
girl (played by Kaitlyn White). This is a great movie for
families.

4. Don't Look in the Attic _____
Rodney Jones and Shontelle Deane star in this scary
new movie. John and Susan are a young husband and
wife who buy a new house. But their beautiful house
has a terrible secret. How can they end their nightmare?
(Don't see this movie alone!)

B Match listings 1–4 with the pictures.

C Read the movie review and add periods, commas, and capital letters.

i saw elizabeth's trip last week it's a really interesting movie and there are some great actors in the cast the movie is about an old woman in new york named elizabeth she wants to visit her grandchildren in los angeles but she's afraid of airplanes she buys a bus ticket and starts an amazing trip she meets a lot of interesting and crazy characters on the bus she also sees some unusual places in the united states i really liked this movie a lot

D Write a review of a new movie. Give your opinion.